Presented To

_____

Date

_____

December 31

Lean in close and listen one more time to what's true...

You are a woman who's loved.

You are a woman who brings joy.

You are a woman who's really going to be okay.

You're Going to Be Okay:
Encouraging Truth Your Heart Needs to Hear, Especially for the Hard Days

Mfd. for © DaySpring Cards, Inc., Siloam Springs, AR 72761.

Text © 2015 Holley Gerth, used under license. www.holleygerth.com

December 30

Because of Jesus, we will be victorious no matter what.

January 1

In this world you will have trouble. But take heart!
I have overcome the world.

JOHN 16:33

December 29

One day we'll be Home.

We'll be with the One we love forever.

January 2

Research shows that almost half of your happiness can be attributed to one factor: you.

December 28

You were faithful over a few things, I will make you ruler over many things. Enter into the joy of your lord.

MATTHEW 25:21

January 3

How you react to life turns out to be far more important than what life throws at you.

December 27

Whatever life brings our way, we can handle it together.

January 4

When you decide to take charge of your heart,
everything changes because *you* change.

December 26

You are a woman of strength. You are a daughter of the King. You are made for a Promised Land.

January 5

You are stronger than you know.

December 25

You're going to be okay.

Not because life is easy.

Not because you have it all together.

Not because everything will work out the way you want.

You're going to make it through this because of
who you are and who you belong to.

January 6

You are loved more than you realize.

December 24

No matter what you're facing, no matter how hard it seems,
no matter how much you feel like giving up on some days,
hold on.

January 7

You are part of a greater plan, and nothing can stop God's purposes for you.

December 23

Hold on to hope.

Hold on to who you are.

Hold on to all God has promised.

January 8

You're going to be okay.

I promise.

And what's even more important: God promises too.

December 22

What has had the most lasting impact on me is that, in the storm and under pressure, God took me to a place of rest, comfort, and ultimately, to a place of absolute beauty. Even among discomfort, disappointment, and displacement, I was kept safe.

—SHEILA WALSH

January 9

Take heart, friend. Good things are ahead.

December 21

But let all who take refuge in you be glad; let them ever
sing for joy. Spread your protection over them,
that those who love your name may rejoice in you.

Surely, Lord, you bless the righteous; you surround them
with your favor as with a shield.

PSALM 5:11-12

January 10

We come to believe that our struggles and circumstances define us. But those are just descriptions, not determinations.

December 20

Simply love. Wherever you are today, with whatever you
have to offer, love and you'll bring greater joy
to your Master and fellow servants than you could ever
even know this side of eternity.

January 11

Who you are doesn't change based on the kind of day,
week, or year you have.

December 19

You don't have to try harder, do more, get better.
You only need to receive God's love and then respond.

That's success.

January 12

You are a daughter of God, a holy princess, a woman loved beyond all you can imagine. *No matter what.*

December 18

It all comes back to love. And love always begins with receiving first. "We love because he first loved us" (1 John 4:19).

January 13

A friend going through a difficult time called me.
As we talked, she kept repeating the same phrase: "I guess
I'm just the girl who has this struggle." I finally stopped her
and said as gently as I could, "That's *where* you're at
right now. It's not *who* you are."

December 17

"Love the Lord your God with all your heart and with all your soul and with all your mind." This is the first and greatest commandment. And the second is like it: "Love your neighbor as yourself."

MATTHEW 22:37-39

January 14

Life's obstacles are temporary. Who you are is eternal.

December 16

To put it simply, *love God and you cannot fail.*
No matter what.

January 15

Our citizenship is in heaven.

PHILIPPIANS 3:20

December 15

You can bring God joy anytime, anywhere,
through anything, and nothing can change that reality.

"We don't have to be a 'citizen' of the 'place' we're standing in right now. I'm not a citizen of Sad City, a resident of Rejectionville, or a townsperson of Trouble Town. I have a citizenship in heaven."

—JENNIFER DUKES LEE

December 14

You never have to compete with
or be compared to anyone.

We all have an equal capacity to bring God joy.

January 17

Your circumstances may change but who you truly are remains forever the same. Your identity is eternally secure in Christ.

December 13

Here's the beautiful truth: nothing can stop you
from being successful. You can bring God joy
in the corner office or in a hospital room. You can bring
him joy changing diapers or changing a church.
You can bring God joy when you're young
and when you're nearing the end of your life.

We can lean into God's heart and ask,
"Who am I *in spite of this?* Tell me what's true
about me no matter what happens."

December 12

That is success, friend.

Being a servant who brings joy to your master.

January 19

It is impossible for God to lie.

HEBREWS 6:18

December 11

What stood out to me this time was one little phrase:
"*enter into* the joy of your lord."

I realized in that moment that God's joy in us
doesn't begin when we get to heaven.
We can live in a way that brings him joy *now*.

January 20

Your circumstances will lie to you. Your emotions will lie to you. Even other people will lie to you. But not God.

December 10

His lord said to him, "Well done, good and faithful servant; you were faithful over a few things, I will make you ruler over many things. Enter into the joy of your lord."

MATTHEW 25:21 NKJV

January 21

We have this hope as an anchor for the soul,
firm and secure.

HEBREWS 6:19

December 9

Adapting to life simply means remaining open
and being willing to try new things. You've done that
again and again throughout your life—
most of the time without even realizing it.
How will tomorrow be different for you?

January 22

Your identity is secure. Nothing going on in your life can change it.

December 8

True service isn't about grand gestures; it's about a series of small choices. Most of them unseen. Many we won't know the impact of this side of heaven. All of which add up to a lifetime of resilience and loving well.

January 23

I am convinced that neither death nor life, neither angels
nor demons, neither the present nor the future,
nor any powers, neither height nor depth, nor anything else
in all creation, will be able to separate us from the love
of God that is in Christ Jesus our Lord.

ROMANS 8:38–39

December 7

Throughout Scripture God uses messy, broken people right in the middle of their greatest challenges. We don't need to have it all together. Wherever we are today, we can serve in some way.

January 24

What the enemy tries to whisper to us
whenever we struggle is this: "If God really loved you,
this wouldn't be happening." In other words, something
is *wrong* with you or everything in your life would be *right*.
But we live in a fallen world. We are broken people.
All of us face hardships and have obstacles to overcome.

December 6

We are made to connect with others.
Daniel Goleman, author of *Social Intelligence*, says,
"Our brain has been preset for kindness."

January 25

Have you believed this lie?

I am not really loved.

If so, then it's time to trade it for the truth.

I am infinitely loved.

December 5

Research has shown that those who have strong relationships and serve others tend to live healthier, more joyful lives.

January 26

God's love is so extraordinary that the psalmist declared it
to be "as high as the heavens are above the earth"
(Psalm 103:11).

December 4

You get to choose how to spend your life. God doesn't have a plan B for you. Being who you are not only makes you resilient—it also changes the world.

January 27

If you need a reminder of God's love,
step outside and try to find the end of the sky.
That's how much you're loved.

December 3

Marcus Buckingham, author of *Find Your Strongest Life*, says it this way:

"Life may ask everything of you, but you cannot do everything. You must learn how to choose, how to focus your life toward specific moments. You must learn how to create more of the strong-moments you want and how to celebrate the ones you have."

January 28

God's love for me doesn't change based on what I accomplish. Instead, it's a free gift.

December 2

Don't let go of your strengths.

Don't let go of your skills.

Don't let go of who God has made you to be.

January 29

We think if we can fix ourselves, then we can fix our lives. But trouble comes to us all. God doesn't promise a problem-free existence. Instead, he offers unconditional love as a shelter for us even on the most difficult of days.

December 1

Because what God has created us to do brings us
so much joy, it can feel self-serving to pursue it
when there seem to be so many other "needs"
in our lives right now. But being who you are truly made
to be is one of the greatest gifts you can offer others,
God, and yourself.

January 30

Taking refuge in God requires *receiving* and not striving.

November 30

My internet connection becomes weaker the farther away from my wireless router I go. In many ways, our hearts are the same. The farther away we get from who God intended us to be, the weaker and more disconnected we feel.

January 31

God transforms all our false beliefs to one simple truth:
If you are mine, you are loved.

November 29

We are each wired by God to fulfill a specific purpose
in this world. He gave us strengths, skills, and
specific people to serve. When we are doing so,
we experience deep fulfillment. When we
move away from that (even without realizing it),
we find our energy and joy beginning to fade.

February 1

You don't have to earn, prove, or strive for anything.

November 28

I've come to believe that optimism is essential
to finishing the race of life well. And by optimism
I don't mean a Pollyanna approach but rather a deep,
abiding faith that God is good and he really will
work out his best for us no matter what.

February 2

No matter what comes your way,
God's love for you doesn't change.

November 27

The authors of *What Happy Women Know* say, "Research suggests that optimists live longer, happier, and more satisfying lives." They also have more good news to share. It turns out optimism can be *learned*.

Being loved is not just a circumstance in your life;
it is who you are.

November 26

How many people do you see who are *truly* living?
You may think those who are have extraordinary genetics
or a lot of luck. But I believe that resilience
is always a choice—and it's always available to us.

February 4

Yes, it's true.

You are loved.

November 25

You can run your race well. You can finish with hope.
You can even dare to enjoy the journey.

February 5

Before you ever came into being,
God had a purpose in mind for you.

November 24

In his book *A Resilient Life*, Gordon MacDonald says, "Too many people see life as a sprint—something fast, furious, quickly finished, bereft of any deep breathing. But life is more than a burst of speed. It is a distance run, and it demands endurance, determination, and a kick at the finish."

February 6

As God alone watched your body being formed
in your mother's womb, he already knew what was ahead.

November 23

I love the word *resilience*. It means that you're able to thrive not just where you are now but for the rest of your life. It means not only can you handle the next step but you can finish well. It means that when you get home to heaven you will hear the words, "Well done, good and faithful servant."

February 7

We are God's handiwork, created in Christ Jesus to do good works, which God prepared in advance for us to do.

EPHESIANS 2:10

November 22

I don't know what your future holds.
But I know Who holds you.

February 8

When life comes along and slaps us silly, it can feel as if God's purpose for us has now been cancelled. But nothing can stop his purposes for us.

November 21

I want to whisper, "I know this isn't easy." You've made it this far, and that tells me so much about you—that you are a brave, beautiful, faithful woman. You are trying to trust even when you're not sure what's ahead. You're persevering when it would be easier to give up.

February 9

Scripture is full of stories in which people found themselves
in difficult circumstances that turned out to be part
of God's mysterious plan.

November 20

David wrote psalms. Jesus spent time
in the wilderness in prayer. Hannah made a trip
to the temple. Paul prayed without ceasing.

God is endless and creative. Why shouldn't
our communication with him be too?

February 10

Joseph's brothers sold him into slavery because of their jealousy. Then his master's wife falsely accused him of rape, so he landed in prison. But God acted on his behalf, and he ended up second in command of the whole country, which enabled him to save the lives of God's people during a famine.

November 19

Jesus said that we don't live on bread alone
but on every word that comes from the mouth of the Lord
(see Matthew 4:4).

February 11

Esther got drafted into the royal harem along with hundreds of other women. Taken away from everything she knew, she had one shot to win the king's favor. She did so and became the next queen, which eventually gave her the opportunity to rescue the Jewish people from the plot of a wicked man.

November 18

Life's storms will come, but the One who calmed the wind and waves can make sure that when the rain ends, you are still standing strong in faith and hope, secure in his arms.

February 12

Jesus himself faced death on a cross and what seemed like the ultimate defeat. Instead of being welcomed as Savior, he experienced betrayal, mistreatment, and abandonment. Yet three days later he victoriously and joyfully rose again to rescue us all from death.

November 17

Jesus *is* the rock. The words he tells us to put into practice aren't just about how we are to live but are about who he is and who we are in him.

February 13

Just because your circumstances are hard
doesn't mean God's purpose for you has changed.

November 16

Therefore everyone who hears these words of mine
and puts them into practice is like a wise man
who built his house on the rock. The rain came down,
the streams rose, and the winds blew and beat
against that house; yet it did not fall,
because it had its foundation on the rock.

MATTHEW 7:24–25

February 14

Joseph, Esther, and even Jesus could have said, "I must have done something wrong. Look at what's happening to me! I'm going to give up and just hang on until heaven." Instead, each one looked past the present and held on to an eternal perspective.

November 15

When nothing makes sense, when all your expectations fall short, when your plans get derailed, there is only One who can offer you a firm foundation for whatever is ahead. When you place your life in God's hands, your future is secure.

February 15

You have not been sidelined.

You have not been disqualified.

You have not been placed on the bench
to wait out the rest of the game.

God's purpose for you *will* prevail.

November 14

How God works is always changing in remarkably creative ways. But his character is firm forever. That means what's most certain about your future is *God himself.*

February 16

In all of history, no person has ever been able to thwart God's ultimate plan.

November 13

What matters most is that our future is secure
not in circumstances but in a Person.

A God who loves you.

A God who holds the world in his hands.

A God who gave his Son for you.

A God who does not change.

February 17

God isn't shocked by the brokenness of this world
or even our personal failures. He can redeem and reroute
as much as is needed to get us to the destination
he has in mind.

November 12

Jesus Christ is the same yesterday and today and forever.

HEBREWS 13:8

February 18

Don't let the enemy lie to you, sister. You have a purpose. Right here, right now. In the middle of all of this.

November 11

God has already given you what is most precious to him,
and that means there is nothing he's not willing to give you.
Does that mean we always get what we want? Nope.
But we can trust that when we don't,
there are greater purposes at work,
and it's not because God is holding out on us.

February 19

You don't have to wait for things to get better.
You don't have to wait until you get your act together.
You don't have to wait until heaven to experience
"life to the full" (see John 10:10).

November 10

He who did not spare his own Son, but gave him up for us all—how will he not also, along with him, graciously give us all things?

ROMANS 8:32

February 20

Here's a secret: we don't have to carry the load of living with purpose. We can embrace it, celebrate it, cling to it—but we don't have to make it happen.

November 9

God had good plans for his Son, but they still included
a cross. We don't escape heartache and trouble in this life.
But we do have the promise that this isn't the end
of the story. God is working out his plan
and nothing can stop him.

February 21

Many are the plans in a person's heart,
but it is the Lord's purpose that prevails.

PROVERBS 19:21

November 8

"For I know the plans I have for you," declares the Lord,
"plans to prosper you and not to harm you,
plans to give you hope and a future."

JEREMIAH 29:11

February 22

Our role is simply to be willing, to open our hands and hearts and say, "God, I'm a mess. My life's a mess. I don't even have a clue what I'm doing. But I'm yours. Thank you for creating me with a purpose. Thank you that nothing and no one can destroy that purpose. Use me."

November 7

God meets our needs as he sees best
and in line with his purposes. That means we don't
always get what we want. God alone knows our hearts,
and he does promise we will always have what we need.

February 23

You are valuable, my friend. Of great worth.
God is going to use you in unexpected, powerful ways.

November 6

My God will meet all your needs according to the riches
of his glory in Christ Jesus.

PHILIPPIANS 4:19

February 24

Over seven billion people inhabit our planet.
But there is only one you. And for as long as the world
continues to exist, that will remain true.

November 5

We will have hard things happen in our lives.
We will face loss. We will be under stress at times.
But God does promise that *who we are* is not changed
by any of this. We will be victorious no matter what.

February 25

God doesn't have a plan B for your life. He doesn't have a backup plan for the gifts he's placed within you. You're our one-shot wonder at getting you.

November 4

In all these things we are more than conquerors
through him who loved us.

ROMANS 8:37

There is only one answer to the question,
"When and where does God want to use me?"
and it's always, "Right now, right here."

November 3

We are not in control. We are not out of control either. We are *in God's control.*

February 27

You may think you have nothing to offer. You may want
to run and hide. You may tell yourself, "I'll only be
in the way." But still God asks, quietly and persistently,
"Will you let me use you, right here and right now?"

November 2

If God is for us, who can be against us?

ROMANS 8:31

February 28

Your weaknesses and struggles are not reasons
for God to give up on you. Instead, they're opportunities
for you to show his strength in ways you simply can't
on your best days.

November 1

God has promised that he will always be with us.
It's okay to ask him to remind you of his love.
"God, I know you're with me. I believe you when you say
that you will never leave me. I feel weak right now. Can you
please help me see one way you're with me today?"

February 29

My strength is made perfect in weakness.

2 CORINTHIANS 12:9 NKJV

October 31

Never will I leave you; never will I forsake you.

HEBREWS 13:5

March 1

The very places and times when you feel God can use you least are when he may actually shine through you most.

We can say, "Lord, I feel fear, but I know you don't want me to stay afraid. Please help me change my thoughts." Our part is fighting that fear and consistently choosing to focus on what God says instead.

March 2

When God uses us in our weak moments,
it's humbling because we realize
it never really has been about us.

October 29

If you're not sure whether what you're doing is worry or wonder and concern, then pause and ask this:
"Am I thinking from a place of fear or a place of faith?"
Most of the time, the answer will be fear. That's okay as a starting point. Then just simply be honest with God.

March 3

We can stop our striving. We can give up working so crazy hard to change the world. We can release our expectations and instead open our hands as well as our plans to God.

October 28

We are to love one another, and that means we will feel *concern* for our brothers and sisters. The difference is that concern ultimately releases people to God, while worry places the burdens of their lives on our shoulders.

March 4

Here is why you are irreplaceable: because you are made in the image of the God who created the universe, and there is a part of who he is that only gets shown through who you are.

October 27

Not worrying doesn't mean we don't think about the future or that we aren't concerned.

We are to *wonder* about the future. That means considering what may be ahead so we can plan wisely.

March 5

Sometimes it's through our cracks
that God's light shines the brightest.

October 26

Jesus said, "You will know the truth, and the truth will set you free" (John 8:32). Jesus also said, "I am the way and the truth and the life" (John 14:6). When he invites us to know the truth, it's not an intellectual invitation. What Jesus is extending here is an invitation to know *him*.

March 6

On your hardest days and in your best moments,
it's still all about God.

October 25

Whisper a prayer like this: "God, thank you
that you are in control, you know everything,
and you have promised to take care of me."

March 7

Offer yourself to God and say, "Lord, I don't know what I have to give right now. I feel empty. I feel broken. I feel weak. But you are in me now just as you are in the times when I feel the strongest and most capable. I want the world to receive what you have designed me to share. I yield myself to you. Use what little I have to make much of you."

October 24

Be transformed by the renewing of your mind.

ROMANS 12:2

March 8

You may have lost some skirmishes,
but that's not who you are.
You're still an overcomer.

October 23

If you know how to worry, then you know how to have hope and faith. It's the same thought pattern with a different focus.

March 9

When we have a weak moment, a bad day, a tough year, the enemy of our souls taunts us. "You've lost," he hisses. But that isn't true. The reality is, *we can't lose*.

October 22

It's okay to have little faith—what matters
is where we're placing whatever faith we do have.

March 10

In all these things we are more than conquerors
through him who loved us.

ROMANS 8:37

October 21

Therefore do not worry about tomorrow,
for tomorrow will worry about itself.
Each day has enough trouble of its own.

MATTHEW 6:34

March 11

Oh, we get knocked around in this life. We have bumps and bruises. Even our Savior left this world with scars. But that doesn't mean we're defeated.

October 20

No matter how many years of Sunday school
we've attended, how often we've watched God move
in our lives, how intellectually certain we are
of what we believe, choosing hope and faith over worry
and fear is something we'll have to do again and again.

March 12

Imagine being a soldier who's going into battle.
Your commander tells you, "We have already won.
All you have to do today is go in there and obey
my commands. Victory is sure." You would fight
with less fear and more faith, less hesitancy
and more certainty, less regret and more intensity.
This is what's true of us.

October 19

God says to his people over and over again,
"Do not be afraid." I love that he uses "be" so often.
To me it says he knows we're tempted to be afraid,
but he's just asking us not to stay that way.
He has a better plan for us instead.

March 13

Life's blows hurt. We ache. We feel the pain.
We are human, and that is inescapable.
Yet we don't have to let our wounds define us.

October 18

The grass isn't greener on the other side.

It's greenest where you help it grow.

March 14

Defeat is not your destiny. You belong to the One
who overcame even death, and that means
there is nothing too difficult for him.

October 17

Jesus knows who you are now
and who you are becoming—and he's committed
to redeeming the changes, all of them,
so that nothing is ever wasted in your life.

March 15

Have you ever heard these thoughts
slip through your mind?

You've let God down.

You should be ashamed of yourself.

How can you not be doing better by now?

Those are the sinister whispers of defeat. And they are lies.

October 16

Jesus understands change is hard. He understands you may not want it. He understands you may wish your circumstances were different.

He knows.

And he knows you.

March 16

God's victory in this world does not depend on you.
It depends on one thing alone: Christ's death on the cross
and resurrection three days later.

October 15

You have what it takes to thrive through change, my friend.

Dare to open your arms and heart to what life brings.

And know that for the parts that are painful, someone else has opened his arms to take the worst of that blow for you. Jesus stretched out on a cross in the ultimate acceptance of change so that he could walk with you and give you life in the middle of everything that comes your way.

March 17

You can't lose the war for God or for yourself.
It's not about you or me at all.
We simply get to partake in the victory.

October 14

Yes, some changes are far more welcome than others.

But none of them is too difficult for God.

And because he lives within you,
none of them is too difficult for you either.

March 18

There is no shame in losing a battle now and then.
It simply means we are imperfect people in a broken world.

October 13

Every time we confront change, it feels like the first time.
And it is, for that particular one. But the pattern of change
is built into who we are as people. We are made to grow.
We are made to overcome obstacles. We are made
to keep moving forward until we're home with Jesus.

March 19

Therefore put on the full armor of God, so that when
the day of evil comes, you may be able to stand
your ground, and after you have done everything, to stand.

EPHESIANS 6:13

October 12

If you are alive and breathing right now, you know how to survive change. The thing is, when we've adjusted to change, we stop calling it "change" and just call it "normal." The changes of yesterday make up the normal of today.

March 20

What we are called to do is simply this: to stand.
Not to conquer the world. Not to be the greatest warrior
ever. Not to never feel weak or afraid. *Just stand.*

October 11

We're not superwomen (and who wants to wear tights all the time anyway?). We're human and we have limits. This is not a sign of weakness; it's a gift because it reminds we are not God.

March 21

Stand on God's promises.

Stand on faith.

Stand on the hope that victory is sure.

October 10

You are not made for passivity and inaction.
Either proactively decide to wait, or take the next step.

March 22

You have already won. You can't be defeated by anything in this life or the next.

You are an overcomer.

October 9

Proverbs 19:21 shows us we are supposed to plan. We are supposed to move forward. And if we happen to go the wrong direction, God is able to redirect us and still get us to his purposes in the end.

March 23

We are *much more* than pretty … we are wonderfully made.

We are *much more* than likeable … we are deeply loved.

We are *much more* than okay … we are daughters of the King.

October 8

Many are the plans in a person's heart,
but it is the Lord's purpose that prevails.

PROVERBS 19:21

March 24

I think the enemy tricks us into believing
we are not enough because he knows
if we discover the truth, we'll be unstoppable.

October 7

The worst decision is no decision at all. If you truly feel that you are to wait, set an amount of time to do so and then reevaluate. Even the Scripture that we like to quote most about waiting—"Be still, and know that I am God" (Psalm 46:10)—involves two proactive phrases: *be still* and *know.*

March 25

As long as we believe we're not enough,
we also believe we have to make up for it.

October 6

Jesus promised the Holy Spirit would
"guide you into all the truth" (John 16:13).

March 26

There is a better way. *Receiving.*
Letting God fill up our "not enough" with his infinite love,
grace, and strength until we're overflowing.

October 5

When you refuse to change, you begin to die
in some small way.

But that doesn't have to happen, because the reverse
is also true. When you embrace change, you begin to live
and grow in some small way—and often in very big ways.

March 27

His divine power has given us everything we need
for a godly life through our knowledge of him
who called us by his own glory and goodness.

2 PETER 1:3

October 4

Look at the world around you: growth and change are the hallmarks of life. The only things in this world that are not growing or changing are not alive.

March 28

In Christ, we have everything we need.
We are all we need to be.

October 3

Ironically, the most powerful freedom turns out to be surrender.

March 29

Instead of asking, "What's wrong with me?" we can ask, "Who's within me?" The answer is an infinite God who knows no limits, who hung the stars in place, who hears our every prayer and directs our every step.

October 2

Our experience of change is transformed when we realize we are not the final decision maker. So we do what we can and then yield as Jesus did in the Garden of Gethsemane: "Not my will, but yours be done" (Luke 22:42).

March 30

God offers a fullness that can't be taken away by bad days, weak moments, or even life's greatest tragedies.

October 1

It's been said that one of the only constants
in our earthly lives is change. It's inevitable, it's continual,
and it can be one of the greatest sources of stress for us.
On the flip side, change is also where we have the most
opportunity to grow and experience God in new ways.

March 31

Yes, we grieve. Yes, we face loss. Yes, we let people down and let people go. But in all of this, who we are is not diminished because the One within us can't be diminished. That never changes, no matter what.

September 30

I can do all this through him who gives me strength.

PHILIPPIANS 4:13

April 1

You are not what happens to you.

You are not where you are right now.

You are not your weakest moments or biggest struggles.

September 29

This is what the Lord says … "I have summoned you by name; you are mine."

ISAIAH 43:1

April 2

You are loved.

You have a purpose.

You are irreplaceable.

You are an overcomer.

You are enough.

September 28

The God who spoke the world into being
has whispered his heart to you too.

April 3

Don't let your circumstances define you.
Instead, hold on to who you really are. To what
God whispers to you. To the identity he's given you
that's eternally unchanging.

September 27

For as high as the heavens are above the earth,
so great is his love for those who fear him.

PSALM 103:11

April 4

You are who God says you are.

And you are *his*—forever.

September 26

What are you afraid to believe but really,
really wish you could?

I'm loved.

I really can do this.

I'm chosen for a purpose.

Whatever it is, it's scandalously true.

April 5

This is the strength you have working within you:
That power is the same as the mighty strength he exerted
when he raised Christ from the dead and seated him
at his right hand in the heavenly realms.

EPHESIANS 1:19–20

September 25

Now I know in part; then I shall know fully,
even as I am fully known.

1 CORINTHIANS 13:12

April 6

The strength within you is the same one that raised Christ from the dead!

September 24

I want to lean in and whisper to you, "Dear sister,
trust that there is more than you can see.
Trust that what you're doing makes a difference."

April 7

God will give us the strength we need
to accomplish his purpose in our lives
regardless of the circumstances.

September 23

We don't have to hurry our growth. In reality,
our striving can no more produce fruit in our lives
than a branch can instantly create a grape. In the end,
we have to yield to greater timelines than our own.

April 8

How God's power and strength uniquely show in you
will never be duplicated by anyone else.

September 22

It seems I most often find Jesus not in the familiar or safe
but just beyond the edge of what I think I can handle.

*Because it's in those moments
I suddenly find he's holding me.*

April 9

You are here, still moving forward,
and asking God to help you.
You are stronger than you know.

September 21

Sometimes our comfort zones are the walls
that block us from God's best for our lives.
When we dare to step beyond them, we open doors
to things we never thought possible.

April 10

Which strengths we display and how we display them
will depend on what we're facing
and God's purposes for us in it.

September 20

Have you ever felt afraid even though you knew
with all your heart you were supposed to do something?
I've found there is only one cure for that kind of fear:
do it anyway.

April 11

Letting God's strength flow through us takes some practice. The apostle Paul said, "*I have learned the secret of being content in any and every situation, whether well fed or hungry, whether living in plenty or in want. I can do all this through him who gives me strength*" (Philippians 4:12–13, emphasis added).

September 19

Wherever you are right now, you're bringing
what God has given you to offer along with you.

April 12

What did Paul need to accomplish God's purpose for his life? Contentment. And how did that happen? Learning.

That means trial-and-error, goof-up-and-ask-forgiveness, give-it-another-shot learning. If Paul needed that process, so do we.

September 18

We're all called to feed the hearts around us.
"Give us today *our* daily bread," says the line
in the Lord's Prayer (Matthew 6:11, emphasis added).
What we receive isn't just for us.

April 13

There is now no condemnation
for those who are in Christ Jesus.

ROMANS 8:1

September 17

God whispers instead to my heart...

"Peace, child, you are loved."

*"Peace, child, you are right in the middle
of my purpose for you."*

"Peace, child, more will come when it is time."

April 14

Ask God to show you how his power
flows through you—even in your weakest moments.
That's how we get stronger.

September 16

Rest is not wasted time.

Rest is preparation.

April 15

God will meet all your needs

PHILIPPIANS 4:19

September 15

We need celebration because it covers our souls, like a red umbrella. Joy stretched out above us, held by unseen hands.

April 16

Be certain of this—God does want you to have human support. Ask him to send you what you need through other people. Even if it's not as soon as you might like, he will answer.

September 14

True success happens when no one is looking, when no one hears, in the quiet of your heart where there's only a divine invitation and an acceptance of it.

April 17

It can be humbling to ask for help,
but now is the time to do it.
Letting others give to you
is a blessing to them as well.

September 13

The moment you say yes to God
and move forward into what he asks of you
is the moment you become successful.

April 18

Sometimes what we see as wasted time is actually the training ground for what God has in store for us. The lessons we learn and the obstacles we overcome are preparation.

September 12

You're stronger than you know. Your God is bigger than you've seen. That hill isn't as unending as it seems right now.

Just keep *going and going and going.*
Until you leave fear and trouble in the dust.

Here's the secret: you're not a quitter … you're a climber.

April 19

The rocks you're struggling to climb over today may be the stepping-stones of tomorrow.

September 11

For the eyes of the Lord range throughout the earth
to strengthen those whose hearts
are fully committed to him.

2 CHRONICLES 16:9

April 20

God never wastes anything.

September 10

I matter to God.

You do too.

We are not unseen.

Not now.

Not ever.

April 21

God is a Redeemer who can transform mistakes.

September 9

Truth doesn't ever go anywhere. But sometimes we lose what we know in the middle of the busy or the hard. Thankfully, we can always go back and what we need is right there waiting for us.

April 22

God won't let this hurt or hard time go unused.

September 8

Surely your goodness and love will follow me all the days of my life, and I will dwell in the house of the Lord forever.

PSALM 23:6

The only difference between a lump of coal and a diamond is time and a lot of pressure.

September 7

Don't settle in the desert.

Don't settle in the hard places.

Don't settle in depression.

Don't settle in fear.

Don't settle anywhere but in the center
of all God has for you.

April 24

God has declared that he is for you.
Everything else you have is from him as well.
But like with Jesus on the cross, the greatest gift
he always offers is himself.

September 6

Solomon, considered the wisest king who ever lived, said,
"I know that there is nothing better for people than
to be happy and to do good while they live. That each
of them may eat and drink, and find satisfaction
in all their toil—this is the gift of God"
(Ecclesiastes 3:12–13).

April 25

El Roi (The God Who Sees, Genesis 16)

There is One who promises his eyes are upon us.
Even when we are in the desert and without hope,
God sees.

September 5

You aren't created to settle. You're created to dwell.

April 26

God doesn't just notice us—*he knows us.*
Deeply, intimately, completely.

September 4

Here's the thing: the fear isn't going away.
You've just gotta do it anyway. One small step at a time.

April 27

Jehovah-Jireh (The Lord Will Provide, Genesis 22)

Need is ultimately a lack of something—time, money, resources, hope, a cure, relationships. Every challenge we face is ultimately about need in some way. God promises to provide all our needs.

September 3

Be careful to obey so that it may go well with you
and that you may increase greatly in a land flowing
with milk and honey, just as the Lord,
the God of your ancestors, promised you.

DEUTERONOMY 6:3

April 28

We can trust that God will provide—not just because he can but because it's *who he is.*

September 2

When that's true and we know what God has asked us to do, obedience is the only way through to the other side.

April 29

Jehovah Rapha (The Lord Who Heals, Exodus 15:22–27)

Whatever you're going through, God knows this:
Yes, we need provision in the desert. But we also need
healing for the barren places of our souls.

September 1

It's not a sign of weakness to need help.
Actually, reaching out is inner strength displayed.

April 30

Jehovah Shalom (The Lord Is Peace, Judges 6)

While external circumstances may be difficult,
it's the inner turmoil that often wears us down most.
We worry. We fret. What God offers instead is peace.
The kind that stays with us no matter what.

August 31

Dare to find the joy where you are now.
Dare to drop your expectations. Dare to believe
that only one thing in your life can be perfect—
and that is the One who gave it to you.

May 1

Jehovah Shammah (The Lord Is There, Ezekiel 48:35)

Because of Jesus, we have hope that whatever we face will not last forever. We can look ahead and know this is certain about our future: the Lord is there.

August 30

Everything in our lives is either out of our grasp
or can be taken from us. Everything but Jesus.
That's a hard truth to hear—but it's a truth
that can set us free from the illusion that if we just
tried harder, earned more, or prayed longer,
then we could have the life we imagine.

May 2

Whatever our circumstances are now, our destiny
is the same. We will one day be with Jesus forever
if we have a personal relationship with him. If you're not
sure that you do, you can change that right now.
Simply stop and pray, "Lord, I know I am a sinner. I need
your forgiveness. Thank you for your death on the cross.
I know that is the only way I can be made right with you.
No matter what has come before in my life, I now
give myself fully and completely to you. Amen."

August 29

Be content with what you have, because God has said,
"Never will I leave you; never will I forsake you."

HEBREWS 13:5

May 3

Moses asks who he should say sent him.
God answers with the name "I am." (Exodus 3:14).

I am is present tense.

I am is here with us.

I am is whatever we need.

I am is a person.

I am is personal.

I am is the answer to our hearts' deepest questions.

August 28

King David says, "*This* is the day the Lord has made; we will rejoice and be glad in it" (Psalm 118:24 NKJV, emphasis added). He doesn't say, "Yesterday was the day the Lord made" or "Tomorrow is the day the Lord will make."

May 4

You have a lot going for you. Even more than you know or can see right now. And you have a great big God who's behind you, beside you, and ahead of you too.

August 27

You are the only you we will ever have. God didn't create a plan B for your life. We need you to be who you are, to do what only you can do. And to do it now, today, in whatever way you can.

May 5

Your eye is the lamp of your body. When your eyes are healthy, your whole body also is full of light. But when they are unhealthy, your body also is full of darkness.

LUKE 11:34

August 26

We don't have to *deserve* joy. It's a fruit of the Spirit.
It's a gift to us as children of God. It's part of our
Promised Land. Joy isn't about being perfect.
It's about being perfectly loved.

May 6

Our perception affects everything. What enables us to truly see the way we're intended? A mind that's filled with light, which means thoughts that line up with truth.

August 25

Joy is something we receive—not something we earn. Yet that doesn't mean it's a passive process. Even when it comes to gifts, there's still action required on our part. We have to be willing to take what's being offered, open it up, and enjoy it.

May 7

We see things not as they are, but as we are ourselves.

—H.M. TOMLINSON

Happiness will not make you selfish.
Instead, it will most likely do just the opposite—
allow you to serve even more out of an overflow.

May 8

Ultimately we are spiritual beings, and that means much of our existence can't be measured or scientifically verified. We do most of our true living within the heart.

August 23

Hebrews 12:2 says we are to live "fixing our eyes on Jesus, the pioneer and perfecter of faith. *For the joy set before him* he endured the cross, scorning its shame, and sat down at the right hand of the throne of God" (emphasis added).

May 9

The joy of the Lord is your strength.

NEHEMIAH 8:10

August 22

Over and over again, research has proven
that the happier you are,
the *more* likely you are to help others.

May 10

What kept me from making changes was the feeling that I wouldn't do it perfectly. I knew I'd still mess up and the changes wouldn't come instantly. Sometimes we girls think if we don't make instant progress, then real change isn't coming. But that's not so. There is a beautiful reality called *imperfect progress*. The day I realized the glorious hope of this kind of imperfect change is the day I gave myself permission to believe I really could be different.

—LYSA TERKEURST

August 21

Author Gretchen Rubin says, "Studies show that happier people are more likely to help other people. They're more interested in social problems. They do more volunteer work and contribute more to charity. Plus, as you'd expect, they're less preoccupied with their personal problems."

May 11

As long as we demand perfection from ourselves, then, ironically, we will make little progress. When we lift those demands, then God can move us forward.

August 20

Jesus said, "I have come that they may have life, and have it to the full" (John 10:10). He didn't say an easy life. He didn't say a self-indulgent life where all your wishes are granted. He didn't say a life free from pain. But he did say a *full* life. One of joy, peace, love, and hope. It's not only possible—it's *promised*.

May 12

Be joyful in hope, patient in affliction, faithful in prayer.

ROMANS 12:12

August 19

Though outwardly we are wasting away,
yet inwardly we are being renewed day by day.

2 CORINTHIANS 4:16

May 13

Gary Oliver likes to say, "If you bury an emotion, you bury it alive." When we avoid what's happening, we eventually face it in another way.

August 18

Because of the myth that the only Promised Land
is in heaven, it seems many Christians accept the desert
as home—as the way it has to be. But that's not true.
You are not made for the desert. I'm not made
for the desert. God has so much more in store for us,
and we don't have to wait until we die to begin receiving it!

May 14

Being patient in affliction means not only persevering
but also devoting the time needed
to really deal with what's happening to us
with the help of God and those who love us.

Happiness doesn't just happen. It's not something
we can sit around and wait to receive. It's not automatic—
quite the opposite. We are fallen people living
in a broken world, and happiness is something
we must be intentional about if we're to experience it.
In many ways, happiness takes hard work.

May 15

More than anything else it is God's help
that makes the difference in difficult situations.

August 16

Like any good father, he experiences joy when his children do too. "May the righteous be glad and rejoice before God; may they be happy and joyful" (Psalm 68:3).

May 16

Being faithful in prayer means
inviting God into our circumstances.

August 15

God is not the cosmic killjoy many of us imagine. All of the evidence points to the opposite. We serve a God of joy, abundance, blessings, and fullness. "The Lord be exalted, who delights in the well-being of his servant" (Psalm 35:27).

May 17

We can say, "God, help me. Be in this with me. Show me what to do."

August 14

If we believe God doesn't want us to have a good life,
then we will stay in places he never intended.
We will settle for less than he has for us. We will make
hard times our identity rather than a stop along the way.

May 18

We do not know what to do, but our eyes are on you.

2 CHRONICLES 20:12

August 13

When you pass through the waters, I will be with you; and when you pass through the rivers, they will not sweep over you. When you walk through the fire, you will not be burned; the flames will not set you ablaze.

ISAIAH 43:2

May 19

We don't have to know the answers.
We don't have to have things figured out.
All we really need to know is where to focus—
and that's on God.

August 12

When God talks about tough places, the words
are temporary. In particular, God uses the word *through*
again and again. For example, the Israelites passed *through*
the Red Sea. They passed *through* the desert.
They eventually passed *through* the Jordan
and into the Promised Land.

May 20

God made us in his image, and he is endlessly creative.
Don't be afraid of trying a new way of talking to him.

August 11

I believed for many years that the Christian life
was all about suffering. But as I look through the pages
of Scripture, I just can't find that to be true.

Yes, we are told we will have trouble and hard times.
We will grieve. We will face loss. We will be disappointed.

But those places of pain are not where we're made
to *dwell*.

May 21

Inviting God into our situations isn't a one-time event. It happens over and over again. And it's not just about speaking our needs to him; it's about listening too.

August 10

God longs to bless us, yearns to bring us joy,
stops at nothing to make sure we have an opportunity
to experience life to the full.

May 22

It takes time to discern God's voice above our emotions and physical reactions. But he is there and promises to guide us through his Spirit.

August 9

Our story begins in a perfect garden.

It takes us to a Promised Land.

It ends with a new heaven and earth.

The heartbeat of God for his people doesn't change from Genesis to Revelation. It's clear he wants us to thrive.

May 23

The point of being transformed in our minds is that
"then you will be able to test and approve
what God's will is—his good, pleasing, and perfect will"
(Romans 12:2).

August 8

Go for it, friend, and let nothing stand in your way—
not even you.

May 24

Finally, brothers and sisters, whatever is true, whatever is noble, whatever is right, whatever is pure, whatever is lovely, whatever is admirable—if anything is excellent or praiseworthy—think about such things.

PHILIPPIANS 4:8

August 7

You make a difference more than you know.
You are called by God and have a purpose that is beyond
what you can even imagine. He has a good plan for you,
and with him you are unstoppable.

May 25

Whatever is true—The first thing to ask ourselves is, "Is this thought true?" Here's the thing: whatever we're thinking *feels* true. It's our internal reality. But that doesn't mean it *actually is* true. Test the thought against Scripture, and if you need to, ask a trusted friend for clarity.

August 6

Be on God's side. And on your side. You are a beautiful, wonderfully created woman with gifts to offer this world.

Whatever is noble, whatever is right—Next we question, "If this is true, is it noble and right?" Noble and right both have meanings associated with moral character. Just because something is factually true doesn't mean it's worthy of our mental attention. In other words, is this thought pleasing to God?

August 5

Paul poses this question: "If God is for us, who can be against us?" (Romans 8:31). The answer should be "no one," but there is one person who can be: you. When we come against ourselves, we side with the enemy.

May 27

Whatever is pure—Even when a thought seems noble, we can ask, "Has anything slipped in to contaminate this thought?" When the enemy tempted Jesus in the wilderness, he didn't use outright lies—he used Scripture out of context. There was some truth but not *pure* truth.

August 4

We are just as capable of supporting ourselves
as we are of being saboteurs. In fact, we're commanded
to love ourselves. Jesus said, "Love your neighbor
as yourself" (Matthew 22:39, emphasis added).

May 28

Whatever is lovely, whatever is admirable—We can ask, "What can I find in my day that is lovely and admirable?" This is about cultivating a habit of looking for the good in life.

August 3

Like it's been for me, guilt may be the gift that has kept on giving in your life. If that's the case, friend, it's time to release it to God. Let him take it away forever. What he's got for you is so much better.

May 29

Whatever is excellent or praiseworthy—We can ask,
"How can I see God's hand in my situation today?"
This takes it one step beyond lovely and admirable.
This is committing to seeing the divine
intersect with our everyday existence
and praising God for it even in the tough times.

August 2

God loves us too much not to tell our hearts when we need to change. He also loves us too much to let us live with guilt.

May 30

It's much easier to just say "whatever" than to practice the "whatevers" given to us in Philippians. But when we choose to practice them, over time our thoughts and lives change for the better.

August 1

When we turn our lives over to God, all our sins are forgiven. And when we mess up (and we will), we can receive more forgiveness. As much as we need.

May 31

The fruit of the Spirit is love, joy, peace, patience, kindness, goodness, faithfulness, gentleness, self-control.

GALATIANS 5:22–23 ESV

July 31

We can never make up for what we've done. We can never cover our debt. We can never earn God's love. *That's exactly why we need a Savior.* Guilt and all our efforts that come from it can never make us right in God's eyes. But the death of Jesus on the cross can.

June 1

Is it a thought that's true, noble, right, pure, lovely, admirable, excellent, or praiseworthy? Is it a thought filled with love, joy, peace, patience, kindness, goodness, faithfulness, gentleness, and self-control?

If the answer is yes, keep on thinking it!

July 30

If we confess our sins, he is faithful and just and will forgive us our sins and purify us from all unrighteousness.

1 JOHN 1:9

June 2

We are human and we all struggle with our thoughts.
That's why "we take captive every thought
to make it obedient to Christ" (2 Corinthians 10:5).

July 29

Guilt is about the law.

We are people of grace.

June 3

I love the word *captive* in 2 Corinthians 10:5
because it shows that God understands
how our thoughts can be like wild little things
that don't do what we'd like at all.

July 28

Here's what I've come to see: *guilt is the modern-day version of trying to make sacrifices for sins.* We mess up and tell ourselves we have to pay somehow. We sacrifice our joy, our worth, even our fellowship with God to show we are sorry.

June 4

We also *make* our thoughts obedient—they don't
do so willingly. One by one we've got to take control
of them, and that takes time, effort, and a lot of practice.

July 27

Draw near to God with a sincere heart
and with the full assurance that faith brings,
having our hearts sprinkled to cleanse us
from a guilty conscience.

HEBREWS 10:22

June 5

"Joy is the most infallible sign of the presence of God."

—ANONYMOUS

July 26

We sabotage ourselves when we take on expectations
because they're simply too much for us to carry.
God invites us to trade those demands for the lightness
of grace and real love instead.

June 6

When we learn how to live with true joy,
we display God in a way that's rare in our world.

July 25

When you feel a weight that's heavy on your shoulders,
pause and ask, "Is this an expectation?"
What's truly from God is not intended to weigh us down.

June 7

Honoring God with our minds isn't easy. It's not instant. But it is possible.

Your mind is a powerful, beautiful gift.

Use it well and wisely, friend.

July 24

God whispers to our hearts, "I know you can't ever
live up to my standards. That's why I sent Jesus.
You are free from striving. You can live in grace, and I will
help you grow. I accept you as you are, and I will be
with you as you joyfully become all I've created you to be."

June 8

Above all else, guard your heart,
for everything you do flows from it.

PROVERBS 4:23

July 23

In place of expectations, Jesus gives us *invitations*.
He tells us, "Come to me, all you who are weary
and burdened, and I will give you rest" (Matthew 11:28).

June 9

When we say what we shouldn't, do what we swore we wouldn't, mess up in more ways than we knew we could, it doesn't begin right at that moment. Those are only outward displays of what's already brewing in our hearts. "The mouth speaks what the heart is full of" (Luke 6:45).

July 22

To be women who live freely, we have to release ourselves and each other from expectations. They are prison bars God never intended for us.

June 10

When our defenses are down in times of stress,
what I really mean is that our hearts are unguarded.
This happens to all of us. It's part of being human.
The good news is that we can learn
how to really guard our hearts.

July 21

Meeting the expectations of others and being loving are two entirely different things. We are never, anywhere in all of Scripture, told to meet the expectations of others.

June 11

Your heart is a treasure. Everything in your life flows from it. It's a wonderful, mysterious gift that God has given you. It holds so much of who you are and what he's called you to do. It's worth protecting.

July 20

I am a servant with one grace-giving master. I'm to love all, but I only have to please One. And that One is not me or anyone else in my life—he's the God who created me.

June 12

All emotions are neutral—even anger, which perhaps gets the worst rap of all. Yes, there are verses like "in your anger do not sin" (Ephesians 4:26). That means we all experience anger—even Jesus did—and what matters is our response to it.

July 19

Living under expectations is like living under the law.
And Jesus has set me free to be a woman of grace.

June 13

By understanding that emotions simply communicate
to us what is happening in our lives,
we can learn to listen to them, express them,
and ask God what he wants us to do.

July 18

Because of Jesus, we don't have to sabotage ourselves. We can live differently. We can get out of our own way.

We need someone to be "Jesus with skin on," as my friend Deidra Riggs likes to say. We are made for connection and community, for authenticity.

July 17

"Who will rescue me from this body that is subject to death?" (Romans 7:24). We need a rescuer. We need someone to save us from ourselves. We need a power greater than our own. Paul knows who that is: "Jesus Christ our Lord!"

June 15

We're never told to let our emotions have mastery over us.
We're to respond with wisdom and kindness. Even research
now verifies that "venting" does more harm than good.
We are to "speak the truth in love" (Ephesians 4:15).

July 16

Thanks be to God, who delivers me
through Jesus Christ our Lord!

ROMANS 7:25

June 16

Your emotions might be saying, "You are unloved,"
but God says, "I have loved you with an everlasting love"
(Jeremiah 31:3).

July 15

We know we have a very real enemy of our souls,
but sometimes it seems the biggest enemy we have to face
is the one staring back at us in the mirror each morning.

June 17

Your emotions might be telling you, "You have completely blown it," but God says, "I work all things together for good for those who love me" (see Romans 8:28).

July 14

The path of the righteous is like the morning sun,
shining ever brighter till the full light of day.

PROVERBS 4:18

June 18

Your emotions might be insisting, "You have no hope,"
but God says, "I have a hope and future for you"
(see Jeremiah 29:11).

July 13

You have a King sitting on the throne of your heart who loves you more than you can even dare to dream. He will take care of you, and he will watch over the secret places of your heart with his love and grace.

June 19

When you experience and express emotions
the way God intended, you are guarding your heart.
You're also guarding your relationships and your very life.

July 12

God is saying, "You can come to me with anything, anytime. Tell me what you need. I will give you peace that's greater than any circumstance.
No matter what happens, I will protect your heart."

June 20

Love One Another (John 13:34)—In our culture,
the word *love* gets tossed around like a football.
We say we love chocolate, television, and our spouses.
Biblical love differs in that it's primarily about action—
the way we treat each other. None of us is perfect,
and we will all mess up at times. But overall,
we are called to love each other well.

July 11

Do not be anxious about anything, but in every situation, by prayer and petition, with thanksgiving, present your requests to God. And the peace of God, which transcends all understanding, will guard your hearts and your minds in Christ Jesus.

PHILIPPIANS 4:6–7

June 21

Be Devoted to One Another (Romans 12:10)—
Devotion is love that hangs in there over time.
It means I'm consistently there for you
and you're there for me. It means I don't give up on you
when a more appealing option comes along.
I'm committed for the ups and downs of our lives.

July 10

None of us lets God have the throne of our hearts
all the time. But at any time we can stop and say,
"God, I have tried to run my own life. I have chased
after idols that can never satisfy. I realize that I am made
to worship, and I want you to be on the throne of my life.
Please take your rightful place. Please guard my heart
and lead my life. Amen."

June 22

Honor One Another (Romans 12:10)—
Honor is essentially respect: it means we act
in ways that show we value each other's time,
gifts, emotions, and other resources.

July 9

If you have children, why do you parent them
rather than letting them do whatever they want?
It's because you love them. It's much the same way
with God. He wants to take care of our hearts,
save us from ourselves, stop us from wasting our lives
chasing after what he knows will ultimately only destroy us.

June 23

Live in Harmony with One Another (Romans 12:16)—
I love the word *harmony* because it's a musical term
about different parts blending together.
We're to share life and appreciate what we have in common
as well as the ways we're uniquely created.

July 8

God isn't on a cosmic power trip. He's not asking for the throne of your life so he can boss you around and make you miserable. He's doing so first because he's God and he rightfully deserves that place. But also because he's the only one who can love you perfectly.

June 24

Accept One Another (Romans 15:7)—
Acceptance transforms our hearts into safe places
where others can grow. Acceptance means I won't
gossip about you, force you to be more like me,
or look down on you. We accept each other because
that is what Jesus did for us.

July 7

Jesus is saying, "Let me be on the throne of your life, and I will give you everything else your heart desires too." Oh, maybe not right away or in the way we expect. But the more we love him, the more our desires align with his, and we finally find the satisfaction we've been so desperately seeking in so many other places.

June 25

Encourage One Another (2 Corinthians 13:11)—
To encourage means "to fill with courage."
We help each other be stronger, go farther, and do more
than we thought we could. When we fall down,
we help each other up. Encouragement lightens our load
and helps us to finish the race God has given us well.

July 6

Jesus invites us to a lifestyle of give-and-take relationships that are led by his Spirit.

June 26

Serve One Another (Galatians 5:13)—It's easy to relate to others in a "what's in it for me?" way. This is actually the natural human response. Instead, Jesus asks us to set that aside and do what he did by serving.

July 5

Seek first his kingdom and his righteousness,
and all these things will be given to you as well.

MATTHEW 6:33

June 27

Be Kind to One Another (Ephesians 4:32)—
Kindness means we practice being sensitive to the needs
of others. We're thoughtful and considerate.
When they're hurting, we seek to comfort them.
When they're rejoicing, we share the joy.

July 4

We all give our devotion to somebody or something.
These impulses are a part of our DNAs, etched into
our natures, as normal and natural as breathing. I believe
they have been placed inside our souls by our Creator God.

Simply put, we are a people wired to worship.
The question isn't, "Do we worship?" The question is,
"Who (or what) do we worship?"

—PETE WILSON

June 28

Part of guarding our hearts is understanding that we simply
can't connect with everyone all the time.
Even Jesus didn't do so.

July 3

THE ONLY WAY WE CAN TRULY LOVE OTHERS

IS TO EXPERIENCE GOD'S LOVE FIRST.

June 29

Jesus had the three closest disciples, then the twelve,
then the forty, and finally the multitudes.
He spent his time and emotional energy effectively.
In other words, he guarded his heart.

July 2

The most important relationship of all is not
one we have with another person.
Instead, it's our connection to God himself.

June 30

Many of us feel guilty because we think
we should be able to love everyone in the same way.
But that's simply not what Jesus asks.

July 1

"One another" is the reality our hearts are made for,
and they thrive most and love best
when that's the way we relate to others.